This Journal
Belongs To:

Taryn E. Smith

(706) 572 - 0534

Now
is the
right time
for an
adventure

Location: _____ Date: _____

Hike/Trail Name: _____

Total Distance/Time: _____

Weather: ☀ ⛅ 🌦 💨 🌧 ⛈ | Temp: _____

Difficulty: 1   2   3   4   5

Description / Comments / Notes for Next Time

_____

_____

_____

_____

_____

_____

_____

Hike Overall Rating

☆ ☆ ☆ ☆ ☆

Location: _____ Date: _____

Hike/Trail Name: _____

Total Distance/Time: _____

Weather: ☀ ⛅ 🌦 💨 🌧 ⛈ | Temp:

Difficulty: 1   2   3   4   5

Description / Comments / Notes for Next Time

_____
_____
_____
_____
_____
_____

Hike Overall Rating
☆ ☆ ☆ ☆ ☆

Location: Clarkesville, Ga   Date:

Hike/Trail Name: Panther Creek

Total Distance/Time: 6miles / 5 hours

Weather: | Temp:

Difficulty: 1   2   3   4   (5)   90°

Description / Comments / Notes for Next Time

More water, lots of hills,
some places no railings,
Some places very steep

Hike Overall Rating

Location: Mt. Airy, Ga   Date:

Hike/Trail Name: Lake Burton

Total Distance/Time: 5 miles / Got lost 6 hrs

Weather: ☀ ⛅ 🌦 💨 🌧 ⛈   Temp:

Difficulty: 1   2   3   (4)   5   85°

Description / Comments / Notes for Next Time

Got lost due to storm damage
No signs or directions

Hike Overall Rating

★ ★ ☆ ☆ ☆

Location: _____, SC_____ Date: _____

Hike/Trail Name: Humphouse Tunnel

Total Distance/Time: 6 miles / All day

Weather: ☀ ⛅ 🌦 ➡ 🌧 ⛈ | Temp: 80's

Difficulty: 1 2 ③ 4 5

Description / Comments / Notes for Next Time

Railroad Trail plus Cave's

Hike Overall Rating

★ ★ ★ ★ ☆

Location: Talluah Falls, Ga Date: _____

Hike/Trail Name: Talluah Falls Gorge

Total Distance/Time: 4 hrs

Weather: ☀️ 🌤️ 🌦️ 💨 🌧️ ⛈️   Temp:

Difficulty: 1 2 3 ④ 5   80's

Description / Comments / Notes for Next Time

lots & lots of stairs
Beautiful view, Lots of people
The state park museum is cool.

Hike Overall Rating

★ ★ ★ ★ ☆

Location: Lavonia, Ga   Date:

Hike/Trail Name: Vogel Park

Total Distance/Time: 1 hr

Weather: ☀ ⛅ 🌦 💨 🌧 ⛈   Temp:

Difficulty: 1 (2) 3 4 5   79 680

Description / Comments / Notes for Next Time

No Directions, Path Destroyed

Hike Overall Rating

⭐ ☆ ☆ ☆ ☆

Location: Clarkesville, Ga   Date: _____

Hike/Trail Name: Old Mill Behind

Total Distance/Time: 1 ¹/₂ miles / 1 hr

Weather: ☀ ⛅ 🌦 💨 🌧 ⛈   Temp: 85°

Difficulty: (1) 2 3 4 5

Description / Comments / Notes for Next Time

Very Beautiful, creeks to play,
Bridges to cross, flowers
everywhere, Birds + lots of
Butterflies

Hike Overall Rating

★ ★ ★ ★ ★

Location: Royston, Ga   Date:

Hike/Trail Name: Victoria State Park

Total Distance/Time: Gave up after 15 min

Weather: ☀ ⛅ 🌦 ⇒ 🌧 ⛈   Temp: 80°

Difficulty: 1   2   3   4   5

Description / Comments / Notes for Next Time

Couldn't find trail
markers or trail
after 15 minutes.
Nice Creek to swim in

Hike Overall Rating

★ ☆ ☆ ☆ ☆

Location: _____ Date: _____

Hike/Trail Name: _____

Total Distance/Time: _____

Weather: ☀ ⛅ 🌦 💨 🌧 ⛈ | Temp:

Difficulty: 1 2 3 4 5

Description / Comments / Notes for Next Time

_____

_____

_____

_____

_____

_____

Hike Overall Rating

☆ ☆ ☆ ☆ ☆

Location: _____ Date: _____

Hike/Trail Name: _____

Total Distance/Time: _____

Weather: ☀ ⛅ 🌦 🌬 🌧 ⛈ | Temp:

Difficulty: 1 2 3 4 5

Description / Comments / Notes for Next Time
_____
_____
_____
_____
_____
_____
_____

Hike Overall Rating
☆ ☆ ☆ ☆ ☆

Location: _____ Date: _____

Hike/Trail Name: _____

Total Distance/Time: _____

Weather: ☀ ⛅ 🌦 💨 🌧 ⛈ | Temp:

Difficulty: 1 2 3 4 5

Description / Comments / Notes for Next Time

_____

_____

_____

_____

_____

_____

Hike Overall Rating

☆ ☆ ☆ ☆ ☆

Location: _____ Date: _____

Hike/Trail Name: _____

Total Distance/Time: _____

Weather: ☀ ⛅ 🌦 🌬 🌧 ⛈ | Temp:

Difficulty: 1 2 3 4 5

Description / Comments / Notes for Next Time

_____

_____

_____

_____

_____

_____

Hike Overall Rating

☆ ☆ ☆ ☆ ☆

Location: _____ Date: _____

Hike/Trail Name: _____

Total Distance/Time: _____

Weather: ☀ ⛅ 🌦 💨 🌧 ⛈ | Temp:

Difficulty: 1 2 3 4 5

Description / Comments / Notes for Next Time

_____

_____

_____

_____

_____

_____

Hike Overall Rating

☆ ☆ ☆ ☆ ☆

Location: _____ Date: _____

Hike/Trail Name: _____

Total Distance/Time: _____

Weather: ☼ ⛅ 🌦 💨 🌧 ⛈ | Temp:

Difficulty: 1 2 3 4 5

Description / Comments / Notes for Next Time

_____

_____

_____

_____

_____

_____

Hike Overall Rating

☆ ☆ ☆ ☆ ☆

Location: _____   Date: _____

Hike/Trail Name: _____

Total Distance/Time: _____

Weather: ☀ ⛅ 🌦 💨 🌧 ⛈   Temp:

Difficulty: 1   2   3   4   5

Description / Comments / Notes for Next Time

_____

_____

_____

_____

_____

_____

_____

Hike Overall Rating

☆ ☆ ☆ ☆ ☆

Location: _____ Date: _____

Hike/Trail Name: _____

Total Distance/Time: _____

Weather: ☀ ⛅ 🌦 💨 🌧 ⛈ | Temp:

Difficulty: 1   2   3   4   5

Description / Comments / Notes for Next Time

_____

_____

_____

_____

_____

_____

Hike Overall Rating

☆ ☆ ☆ ☆ ☆

Location: _____ Date: _____

Hike/Trail Name: _____

Total Distance/Time: _____

Weather: ☀ ⛅ 🌦 💨 🌧 ⛈ | Temp: _____

Difficulty: 1 2 3 4 5

Description / Comments / Notes for Next Time

_____

_____

_____

_____

_____

_____

Hike Overall Rating

☆ ☆ ☆ ☆ ☆

Location: _____ Date: _____

Hike/Trail Name: _____

Total Distance/Time: _____

Weather: ☀ ⛅ 🌦 💨 🌧 ⛈ | Temp:

Difficulty: 1 2 3 4 5

Description / Comments / Notes for Next Time

_____

_____

_____

_____

_____

_____

Hike Overall Rating

☆ ☆ ☆ ☆ ☆

Location: _____   Date: _____

Hike/Trail Name: _____

Total Distance/Time: _____

Weather: ☀ ⛅ 🌦 💨 🌧 ⛈   Temp:

Difficulty: 1   2   3   4   5

Description / Comments / Notes for Next Time

_____

_____

_____

_____

_____

_____

Hike Overall Rating

☆ ☆ ☆ ☆ ☆

Location: _____ Date: _____

Hike/Trail Name: _____

Total Distance/Time: _____

Weather: ☀ ⛅ 🌦 💨 🌧 ⛈ | Temp:

Difficulty: 1 2 3 4 5

Description / Comments / Notes for Next Time

_____

_____

_____

_____

_____

_____

Hike Overall Rating

☆ ☆ ☆ ☆ ☆

Location: _____ Date: _____

Hike/Trail Name: _____

Total Distance/Time: _____

Weather: ☀ ⛅ 🌦 💨 🌧 ⛈ | Temp:

Difficulty: 1   2   3   4   5

Description / Comments / Notes for Next Time

_____

_____

_____

_____

_____

Hike Overall Rating

☆ ☆ ☆ ☆ ☆

Location: _____ Date: _____

Hike/Trail Name: _____

Total Distance/Time: _____

Weather: ☀ ⛅ 🌦 💨 🌧 ⛈ | Temp:

Difficulty: 1 2 3 4 5

Description / Comments / Notes for Next Time

_____

_____

_____

_____

_____

_____

Hike Overall Rating

☆ ☆ ☆ ☆ ☆

Location: _____ Date: _____

Hike/Trail Name: _____

Total Distance/Time: _____

Weather: ☀ ⛅ 🌦 💨 🌧 ⛈ | Temp:

Difficulty: 1 2 3 4 5

Description / Comments / Notes for Next Time

_____

_____

_____

_____

_____

_____

_____

Hike Overall Rating

☆ ☆ ☆ ☆ ☆

Location: _____ Date: _____

Hike/Trail Name: _____

Total Distance/Time: _____

| Weather: ☀ ⛅ 🌦 🌬 🌧 ⛈ | Temp: |
| Difficulty: 1 2 3 4 5 | |

Description / Comments / Notes for Next Time

_____

_____

_____

_____

_____

_____

Hike Overall Rating

☆ ☆ ☆ ☆ ☆

Location: _____   Date: _____

Hike/Trail Name: _____

Total Distance/Time: _____

Weather: ☀ ⛅ 🌦 🌬 🌧 ⛈ | Temp:

Difficulty: 1   2   3   4   5

Description / Comments / Notes for Next Time

_____

_____

_____

_____

_____

_____

Hike Overall Rating

☆ ☆ ☆ ☆ ☆

Location: _____ Date: _____

Hike/Trail Name: _____

Total Distance/Time: _____

Weather: ☀ ⛅ 🌦 🌬 🌧 ⛈	Temp:
Difficulty: 1 2 3 4 5	

Description / Comments / Notes for Next Time

_____

_____

_____

_____

_____

_____

Hike Overall Rating

☆ ☆ ☆ ☆ ☆

Location: _____ Date: _____

Hike/Trail Name: _____

Total Distance/Time: _____

Weather: ☀ ⛅ 🌦 💨 🌧 ⛈ | Temp:

Difficulty: 1   2   3   4   5

Description / Comments / Notes for Next Time

_____

_____

_____

_____

_____

_____

Hike Overall Rating

☆ ☆ ☆ ☆ ☆

Location: _____ Date: _____

Hike/Trail Name: _____

Total Distance/Time: _____

Weather: ☀ ⛅ 🌦 💨 🌧 ⛈ | Temp: _____

Difficulty: 1 2 3 4 5

Description / Comments / Notes for Next Time

_____

_____

_____

_____

_____

_____

Hike Overall Rating

☆ ☆ ☆ ☆ ☆

Location: _____ Date: _____

Hike/Trail Name: _____

Total Distance/Time: _____

Weather: ☀ ⛅ 🌦 💨 🌧 ⛈ | Temp:

Difficulty: 1 2 3 4 5

Description / Comments / Notes for Next Time

_____
_____
_____
_____
_____
_____

Hike Overall Rating

☆ ☆ ☆ ☆ ☆

Location: _____ Date: _____

Hike/Trail Name: _____

Total Distance/Time: _____

Weather: ☀ ⛅ 🌦 💨 🌧 ⛈ | Temp:

Difficulty: 1   2   3   4   5

Description / Comments / Notes for Next Time

_____

_____

_____

_____

_____

_____

Hike Overall Rating

☆ ☆ ☆ ☆ ☆

Location: _____ Date: _____

Hike/Trail Name: _____

Total Distance/Time: _____

Weather: ☀ ⛅ 🌦 🌬 🌧 ⛈   Temp:

Difficulty: 1   2   3   4   5

Description / Comments / Notes for Next Time

_____

_____

_____

_____

_____

_____

Hike Overall Rating

☆ ☆ ☆ ☆ ☆

Location: _____ Date: _____

Hike/Trail Name: _____

Total Distance/Time: _____

Weather: ☀ ⛅ 🌦 💨 🌧 ⛈ | Temp:

Difficulty: 1   2   3   4   5

Description / Comments / Notes for Next Time

_____

_____

_____

_____

_____

_____

Hike Overall Rating

☆ ☆ ☆ ☆ ☆

Location: _____ Date: _____

Hike/Trail Name: _____

Total Distance/Time: _____

Weather: ☀ ⛅ 🌦 💨 🌧 ⛈ | Temp:

Difficulty: 1   2   3   4   5

Description / Comments / Notes for Next Time

_____

_____

_____

_____

_____

_____

Hike Overall Rating

☆ ☆ ☆ ☆ ☆

Location: _____ Date: _____

Hike/Trail Name: _____

Total Distance/Time: _____

Weather: ☀ ⛅ 🌦 🌬 🌧 ⛈ | Temp:

Difficulty: 1   2   3   4   5

Description / Comments / Notes for Next Time

_____

_____

_____

_____

_____

_____

Hike Overall Rating

☆ ☆ ☆ ☆ ☆

Location: _____ Date: _____

Hike/Trail Name: _____

Total Distance/Time: _____

Weather: ☀ ⛅ 🌦 💨 🌧 ⛈ | Temp:

Difficulty: 1   2   3   4   5

Description / Comments / Notes for Next Time

_____

_____

_____

_____

_____

_____

Hike Overall Rating

☆ ☆ ☆ ☆ ☆

Location: _____ Date: _____

Hike/Trail Name: _____

Total Distance/Time: _____

Weather: ☀ ⛅ 🌦 💨 🌧 ⛈	Temp:
Difficulty: 1 2 3 4 5	

Description / Comments / Notes for Next Time

_____

_____

_____

_____

_____

Hike Overall Rating

☆ ☆ ☆ ☆ ☆

Location: _____ Date: _____

Hike/Trail Name: _____

Total Distance/Time: _____

Weather: ☀ ⛅ 🌦 💨 🌧 ⛈ | Temp:

Difficulty: 1   2   3   4   5

Description / Comments / Notes for Next Time

_____

_____

_____

_____

_____

_____

Hike Overall Rating

☆ ☆ ☆ ☆ ☆

Location: _____ Date: _____

Hike/Trail Name: _____

Total Distance/Time: _____

Weather: ☀ ⛅ 🌦 🌬 🌧 ⛈ | Temp:

Difficulty: 1   2   3   4   5

Description / Comments / Notes for Next Time

_____

_____

_____

_____

_____

_____

Hike Overall Rating

☆ ☆ ☆ ☆ ☆

Location: _____ Date: _____

Hike/Trail Name: _____

Total Distance/Time: _____

Weather: ☀ ⛅ 🌦 💨 🌧 ⛈ | Temp: _____

Difficulty: 1   2   3   4   5

Description / Comments / Notes for Next Time

_____

_____

_____

_____

_____

_____

_____

Hike Overall Rating

☆ ☆ ☆ ☆ ☆

Location: _____ Date: _____

Hike/Trail Name: _____

Total Distance/Time: _____

Weather: ☀ ⛅ 🌦 💨 🌧 ⛈ | Temp:

Difficulty: 1 2 3 4 5

Description / Comments / Notes for Next Time

_____

_____

_____

_____

_____

_____

Hike Overall Rating

☆ ☆ ☆ ☆ ☆

Location: _____ Date: _____

Hike/Trail Name: _____

Total Distance/Time: _____

Weather: ☀ ⛅ 🌦 💨 🌧 ⛈ | Temp:

Difficulty: 1   2   3   4   5

Description / Comments / Notes for Next Time

_____

_____

_____

_____

_____

Hike Overall Rating

☆ ☆ ☆ ☆ ☆

Location: _____ Date: _____

Hike/Trail Name: _____

Total Distance/Time: _____

Weather: ☀ ⛅ 🌦 💨 🌧 ⛈ | Temp:

Difficulty: 1 2 3 4 5

Description / Comments / Notes for Next Time

_____

_____

_____

_____

_____

_____

Hike Overall Rating

☆ ☆ ☆ ☆ ☆

Location: _____ Date: _____

Hike/Trail Name: _____

Total Distance/Time: _____

Weather: ☀ ⛅ 🌦 💨 🌧 ⛈ | Temp:

Difficulty: 1   2   3   4   5

Description / Comments / Notes for Next Time

_____

_____

_____

_____

_____

_____

Hike Overall Rating

☆ ☆ ☆ ☆ ☆

Location: _____ Date: _____

Hike/Trail Name: _____

Total Distance/Time: _____

Weather: ☀ ⛅ 🌦 💨 🌧 ⛈ | Temp:

Difficulty: 1 2 3 4 5

Description / Comments / Notes for Next Time

_____

_____

_____

_____

_____

_____

Hike Overall Rating

☆ ☆ ☆ ☆ ☆

Location: _____ Date: _____

Hike/Trail Name: _____

Total Distance/Time: _____

| Weather: ☀ ⛅ 🌦 🌬 🌧 ⛈ | Temp: |
| Difficulty: 1 2 3 4 5 | |

Description / Comments / Notes for Next Time

_____

_____

_____

_____

_____

_____

Hike Overall Rating

☆ ☆ ☆ ☆ ☆

Location: _____ Date: _____

Hike/Trail Name: _____

Total Distance/Time: _____

Weather: ☀ ⛅ 🌦 💨 🌧 ⛈ | Temp:

Difficulty: 1 2 3 4 5

Description / Comments / Notes for Next Time

_____

_____

_____

_____

_____

_____

Hike Overall Rating

☆ ☆ ☆ ☆ ☆

Location: _____ Date: _____

Hike/Trail Name: _____

Total Distance/Time: _____

Weather: ☀ ⛅ 🌦 💨 🌧 ⛈ | Temp:

Difficulty: 1 2 3 4 5

Description / Comments / Notes for Next Time

_____

_____

_____

_____

_____

_____

_____

Hike Overall Rating

☆ ☆ ☆ ☆ ☆

Location: _____ Date: _____

Hike/Trail Name: _____

Total Distance/Time: _____

Weather: ☼ ⛅ 🌦 💨 🌧 ⛈ | Temp:

Difficulty: 1   2   3   4   5

Description / Comments / Notes for Next Time

_____

_____

_____

_____

_____

_____

Hike Overall Rating

☆ ☆ ☆ ☆ ☆

Location: _____   Date: _____

Hike/Trail Name: _____

Total Distance/Time: _____

Weather: ☀ ⛅ 🌦 🌬 🌧 ⛈ | Temp:

Difficulty: 1   2   3   4   5

Description / Comments / Notes for Next Time

_____

_____

_____

_____

_____

_____

Hike Overall Rating
☆ ☆ ☆ ☆ ☆

Location: _____ Date: _____

Hike/Trail Name: _____

Total Distance/Time: _____

Weather: ☀ ⛅ 🌦 💨 🌧 ⛈ | Temp:

Difficulty: 1 2 3 4 5

Description / Comments / Notes for Next Time

_____

_____

_____

_____

_____

_____

Hike Overall Rating

☆ ☆ ☆ ☆ ☆

Location: _____ Date: _____

Hike/Trail Name: _____

Total Distance/Time: _____

Weather: ☀ ⛅ 🌦 💨 🌧 ⛈ Temp:

Difficulty: 1 2 3 4 5

Description / Comments / Notes for Next Time

_____

_____

_____

_____

_____

_____

Hike Overall Rating

☆ ☆ ☆ ☆ ☆

Location: _____ Date: _____

Hike/Trail Name: _____

Total Distance/Time: _____

Weather: ☀ ⛅ 🌦 🌬 🌧 ⛈ | Temp:

Difficulty: 1 2 3 4 5

Description / Comments / Notes for Next Time

_____

_____

_____

_____

_____

_____

Hike Overall Rating

☆ ☆ ☆ ☆ ☆

Location: _____ Date: _____

Hike/Trail Name: _____

Total Distance/Time: _____

Weather: ☀ ⛅ 🌦 💨 🌧 ⛈ | Temp:

Difficulty: 1   2   3   4   5

Description / Comments / Notes for Next Time

_____

_____

_____

_____

_____

_____

Hike Overall Rating

☆ ☆ ☆ ☆ ☆

Location: _____ Date: _____

Hike/Trail Name: _____

Total Distance/Time: _____

Weather: ☼ ⛅ 🌦 💨 🌧 ⛈ | Temp: _____

Difficulty: 1   2   3   4   5

Description / Comments / Notes for Next Time

_____

_____

_____

_____

_____

_____

Hike Overall Rating

☆ ☆ ☆ ☆ ☆

Location: _____ Date: _____

Hike/Trail Name: _____

Total Distance/Time: _____

Weather: ☀ ⛅ 🌦 💨 🌧 ⛈ | Temp:

Difficulty: 1   2   3   4   5

Description / Comments / Notes for Next Time

_____

_____

_____

_____

_____

_____

Hike Overall Rating

☆ ☆ ☆ ☆ ☆

Location: _____ Date: _____

Hike/Trail Name: _____

Total Distance/Time: _____

Weather: ☀ ⛅ 🌦 💨 🌧 ⛈ | Temp:

Difficulty: 1 2 3 4 5

Description / Comments / Notes for Next Time

_____

_____

_____

_____

_____

_____

Hike Overall Rating

☆ ☆ ☆ ☆ ☆

Location: _____ Date: _____

Hike/Trail Name: _____

Total Distance/Time: _____

| Weather: ☀ ⛅ 🌦 💨 🌧 ⛈ | Temp: |
| Difficulty: 1 2 3 4 5 | |

Description / Comments / Notes for Next Time

_____

_____

_____

_____

_____

_____

_____

Hike Overall Rating

☆ ☆ ☆ ☆ ☆

Location: _____ Date: _____

Hike/Trail Name: _____

Total Distance/Time: _____

Weather: ☀ ⛅ 🌦 💨 🌧 ⛈ | Temp:

Difficulty: 1   2   3   4   5

Description / Comments / Notes for Next Time

_____

_____

_____

_____

_____

_____

Hike Overall Rating

☆ ☆ ☆ ☆ ☆

Location: _____ Date: _____

Hike/Trail Name: _____

Total Distance/Time: _____

Weather: ☀ ⛅ 🌦 💨 🌧 ⛈ | Temp: _____

Difficulty: 1   2   3   4   5

Description / Comments / Notes for Next Time

_____

_____

_____

_____

_____

_____

Hike Overall Rating

☆ ☆ ☆ ☆ ☆